The Dream is Gone

Economic Survival in 21st Century America

Say No to Credit – Say No to Banks

by

Ron Charleston

Disclaimer

Although the author and publisher have made every effort to ensure that the information in this book was correct at press time, the author and publisher do not assume and hereby disclaim any liability to any party for any loss, damage, or disruption caused by errors or omissions, whether such errors or omissions result from negligence, accident, or any other cause.

Table of Contents

ACKNOWLEDGMENTS

A big thank you to my publisher for helping me put this together.

Introduction

At one time, I had a very good paying job, but like so many other Americans have experienced, my job was outsourced to China. I was a middle-aged man with skills that were no longer needed, at least for a person my age. I soon learned how difficult it was for older people, even those in their mid 40s, to find employment. But I did find work, just not what I wanted, and certainly not at the wages I was used to.

I felt I was too old to begin a new career, and so I went from one job to another, trying to survive. During this time I slowly began accumulating debt. Eventually, my efforts led to a life of self-employment, with several different sources of income. No single source of income was ever sufficient to live on, but taken in total, I was able to get out of debt and live comfortably.

For many Americans, it may seem like we are moving rapidly out of the middle class and towards poverty. This is not just a feeling. The middle class is disappearing, and you need to take steps now to insure your economic survival, today and in the future.

Today's America is different than it has been in the past. Regardless of the propaganda on television about the American dream, the agenda for the average American is survival. This book contains the hard lessons I have learned about economic survival in 21st century America.

This book is written for those who see their standard of living shrink. I hope the lessons contained in these pages will help you to hold on to your quality of life as our country's middle class continues to decline.

Section 1

No more credit

You need to be debt free

The numbers for average household debt in the United States can be tricky to calculate, and unless you break down the data into different categories, the numbers will have no meaning to anyone. The average credit card debt per household was $15,191 in 2014, but this is deceptive. At any given time, an individual can have a balance owed on their credit card, but they pay it off every month. Others may have their accounts near the credit limit. This latter type of consumer will be making payments on an outstanding balance with most of the money going towards interest. The average interest rate on a credit card in 2014 was 14.95% APR. Those who pay off their balance each month are usually the ones with lower interest rates, but credit card companies make the bulk of their profits from high interest charges for people who carry a balance. If you are one of these people, you need to make changes quickly, and free yourself from the bondage of lenders.

And make no mistake, owing money is a type of bondage. To make matters worse, for most people debt creates more debt. As your debt grows, you find more and more of your paycheck spent on payments toward your debt, and a portion of this money will go towards interest on your debt. You end up living below your income because so much of your money is spent on something you purchased in the past, plus the interest for borrowing the money.

Of course, if you are in debt, I'm not telling you anything you don't already know, but in the economy today and into the future, your debt is going to become an even bigger problem. One, your income may drop because you may be next to lose your job. How are you going to pay your debts without a job? If creditors are not hounding you today, they will be when you get a pink slip. The stress of unemployment is high; you don't need debts hanging over your head during this time as well.

A second problem with debt is the global problem of deflation. You may be familiar with inflation, but deflation is the exact opposite and can be a big problem for debtors. Inflation is when you go to bed at night with a dollar in your pocket, and the next morning it is worth $0.95. Deflation is the when you go to bed at night and wake up the next morning and your dollar is worth $1.05. This is exaggerated to illustrate the concept, but what this means is that you will, in effect, owe even more money than you did before. In a deflationary world, cash is king, and debt is even more expensive than ever before.

Although getting out of debt is a strong move to defend yourself from the economic assault so many of us feel, you must stay out of debt. I do not believe that credit serves any purpose to an individual. Its only purpose is to increase profits for businesses.

Companies want you in debt

Corporations do everything they can to get your signature on the dotted line for a credit card or to finance any number of large purchases. If you cannot afford to buy on credit, they don't care; that is your problem. You shouldn't have borrowed the money if you couldn't afford to pay it back. That is what you're told. Of course, it is no holds barred to get you in debt in the first place, and there is no such thing as predatory lending. The loan contract will always favor the lender. And yes, you should have read the entire contract before signing it, but try to do that in real life. The pressure can be intense, especially if the loan is for a car. Sometimes there is no pressure; just a slick finance officer or salesman distracting you from the paperwork that will be a long-term implication for your personal finances.

There is no benefit to consumer debt

The talking heads on television will always preach the importance of a good credit rating, so you can buy a home someday. Notice how you need to be paying on a mortgage for a house to have a home. Real estate propaganda aside, a home is where you are with your family and friends. It doesn't matter whether you are renting or buying. Of course, since the collapse of the housing market with the mortgage fiasco on Wall Street, it is difficult to talk about the need for good credit to buy a house. Now, they speak of the need for a good credit score to rent or get a job. They actually say this with a straight face. Seriously, the only reason you don't have the job you want or need is because of your credit score. And, of course, homeless people all over the nation are in the condition they are in because of a poor credit rating.

Avoid new debt like the plague

Corporations want to extract as much money from you as they possibly can, and if you don't have any money, they are usually willing to take a portion of your future earnings. If it were legal, they might even take your first born.

The solution to this problem, of course, is to simply buy nothing on credit. This is contrary to everything you will hear on television and the radio, but this is understandable. The media gets its revenue from advertisers, and without exception, these are commercial enterprises. Businesses that are attempting to make a profit and advertising on television will produce commentary with opinions that, at the least, will not criticize the hand that feeds them. At worst, they will echo the propaganda from big business, and there is no greater propaganda than the need for a good credit rating.

No payday loans! They are legal loan sharks

When I was a boy growing up, there were people who loaned money illegally. They were called loan sharks. The nickname came from the fact that they would charge interest rates that were considered usury; therefore, they were against the law. In the movies and on television, they were portrayed as men who would send a thug over to your home to break your leg or arm if you didn't pay when the money was due. Although it is true that loan sharks existed, they seldom were violent. In most cases, they would carry the loan over for another week or two and charge more interest. People would become in debt to these men, and it would be difficult to ever pay them back.

Today, you seldom hear about loan sharks because it has become legal in most states. At the time of this writing, loan sharking is legal in 37 of the 50 states. Of course, it is not called loan sharking. Now, the business is called payday lending! It is a legitimate industry, at least in the sense that it is legal, but just because something is legal doesn't make it right. Payday lenders will loan money for a week to 30 days and at interest rates that would have made a loan shark embarrassed. Payday lenders have put loan sharks out of business.

Payday lenders flourish in areas of high unemployment and poverty, and like loan sharks, they get their customers hooked on their lending service. They advertise their services as getting money fast and easy. Two words that are appealing to cash strapped Americans. Most people can qualify for this type of loan because there is no credit check. All the payday lender wants to know is that you have a steady job and a bank account. There is no need for collateral. They will collect their money, with interest, on your payday, just like a loan shark would have done. In some cases, they will take the money directly from your bank account while other lenders may take a post dated check from you. In either case, if it looks like you won't have all of the money on payday, the loan can be extended, with additional fees.

The average person does not understand how outrageous the interest rates are, and even when the payday lender is required by state law to display them, they will also list their fees. This is the same as interest, but it is simpler to comprehend. A person borrows a hundred dollars and pays back $125 in four weeks. This is easy to understand, but also represents over 600 percent annual interest. Years ago, men caught lending like this went to jail.

Studies have shown that the average customer owes money five months out of the year to payday lenders, and because of fees and interest, they end up paying two and a half times the money they borrowed.

Do not borrow money from these people. Your ultimate goal should be to never borrow again, but the first place to start is with the payday lenders.

Do you really need a credit card?

There are many people who claim that everyone needs a credit card, you just need to learn to use it responsibly. They will say there are many good reasons to have a credit card. They are safer than cash, or you need to have at least one for a financial emergency. You also need them to help build your credit rating, and some will tell you that a credit card is mandatory for certain purchases. There are even those who will tell you that credit cards, when used properly, are financially profitable. Let's look at each one of these reasons.

They are safer than carrying cash and offer protection from theft

No kidding. But the truth is a debit card is just as safe. If your debit card is lost or stolen, you can have it replaced, and if someone gets a hold of your card number and starts making charges, you will be protected. I had this happen to me. I had my debit card number somehow compromised, and there were charges at a gas station in Brooklyn, New York. I was living on the west coast at the time, and I had never been anywhere in New York in my life. The charges on my debit card were reversed, and it didn't cost me any money.

You need to have at least one credit card in a financial emergency

You need a savings to fall back on and not a line of credit. One of the ideas behind this book is to turn your back on credit and begin to achieve independence with a surplus in cash.

You need them to help build your credit rating

A good credit rating means that you have the privilege of paying more for something than you could have paid with cash.

They are mandatory for certain services

There are two primary examples of this. One is renting cars; the other is hotel rooms. In both situations, the business does not know what your final bill will be, and they also need to protect themselves from damages. With a credit card, they will first block off a certain amount of money, and then when the final bill is known, they will charge this amount to your credit card. This is usually a lower amount than the initial amount they reserved on your card. But a company can do the same thing with a debit card. You only need to make sure you have enough on your debit card for the reserve until the final bill. The bottom line is that you can use a debit card with certain rental agencies and hotels. You need to call ahead to find out who will take a debit card, and if so, how much they will reserve on your card. You will run into a few companies that won't take a debit card, but this is a small price to pay for financial freedom.

Credit cards are financially profitable

There are many people who like the idea of cash back when using a credit card, but this usually doesn't make financial sense unless you have a card with no annual fee, and you never carry a balance. Only people of large financial means fall into this category. For the rest of us, having a credit line is too much temptation. Besides, there are debit cards that offer cash back on signature purchases.

My final thought on credit cards

The problem with credit cards is not the responsible versus irresponsible use of them, but a problem with using them at all. You don't need a credit card. If you don't want to carry any cash, you can use a debit card.

Never mind your credit rating

If you turn on television and listen to personal finance gurus, they always tell you that your credit rating is extremely important. They are partly right. Although it is true that good credit is better than bad credit, there is a third type of credit that is best of all – NO CREDIT! Unfortunately, in American society, we are drenched with advertisements about buying on credit as well as propaganda about the importance of good credit rating. If we maintain a good credit rating, we will be rewarded by paying lower interest rates on future purchases. This is big business at its best, but it benefits the corporation and not the consumer. Do not fall into the debt trap. There is no reason to ever use credit, especially credit cards; they are a sucker's game.

If you are not in debt, do not start now. If you have any debt and it is manageable, you need to think about paying it off as soon as possible. In the long run, you will be better off. However, if you have a lot of debt and are not sure what to do about it, then read the next section.

Section 2

Get Out of Debt Starting Right Now

Personal Debt

If you are in debt, you need to get rid of this financial and emotional nuisance as soon as possible. Never mind your credit rating. Do whatever it takes to become debt free and never borrow again. There is no financial advantage to be had with debt. In years past, there would be people who would talk about good debt and bad debt. Of course, good debt was money borrowed for investment purposes and was usually a mortgage for a home. We learned in 2008, when the real estate bubble collapsed, that you can lose a great deal of money by having a mortgage. But even now, there are those who would make an argument to have a mortgage versus renting, and some of these people can make a good argument. I sit on the fence with this issue, but if you can pay a mortgage, plus property taxes and upkeep of the home and this amount of money is roughly the same or close to renting, then perhaps it is a good idea. But even in this case, you should only see a mortgage as being cheaper than renting, and not consider it an investment.

The mortgage issue aside, personal debt is evil. Never borrow to pay for anything. Whatever debts you have, you need to create a plan to get yourself out of debt. There are three good approaches to take, but which one is best for you is dependent upon your current financial situation. The first step is to figure out where you are right now. Write down all of your income for a given month, and then write down all of your monthly expenses. Remember to include those yearly expenses as well. Things such as car registration, you can simply divide by 12. Once you have this number, subtract it from your monthly income. If you are negative, you may want to consider bankruptcy. However, before doing this, look at any assets that you have that are not related to your retirement, your house or children's education. If you have any assets left that are not being held as security for a loan, you might want to consider selling these items and pay down your debt. The idea, of course, is to get your monthly debt below your income. If this is not possible, you should consult a bankruptcy attorney.

Section 3

Two Paths to Avoid Bankruptcy

If the numbers show that you are not close to a bankruptcy, you can consider taking one of two paths: a debt consolidation loan or paying back the debt yourself, using a method such as the snowball strategy for debt repayment.

A debt consolidation loan

It is possible to get a single loan that is used to pay off all of your debts, and then make a single payment to one lender. If your debts are not too great, it may be possible to get a loan without any collateral. The advantage to this type of loan is that you are able to make a single payment each month instead of spreading out your payments to several creditors. When you spread your payments out, you end up paying for a lot of interest and make little progress in paying down the principle. This is especially true when it is credit card debt.

A debt consolidation loan, to be effective, will be closed ended. This simply means that the loan is calculated based upon principle and interest and is divided up into a fixed number of payments. Once these payments are completed, the loan is paid off. This type of loan should also offer a smaller payment than the total of the minimum payments on all of your other debts. This will give you extra money each month as you pay down your debt.

Although this type of loan may seem attractive, there are pitfalls involved. This type of loan will only help if you maintain the discipline to make your payments on time and do not borrow any more money. This means not using any type of credit, but if you have been moved by my sermon in section one on this topic, this should not be an issue for you.

One thing you should avoid is using the equity in your home as collateral to consolidate credit debt. When you do this, you are switching from unsecured debt to a collateralized loan, and this will benefit lenders more than it ever does consumers.

The Snowball Method

This method has been around for awhile, but many people do not know about it. Basically, you write down all of your debts on a piece of paper along with the minimum payments needed each month. Take your extra money that you have each month, and apply it to one of these debts while paying the minimums on the others. As soon as you have paid off the first debt, take all of the money you were applying to it and combine it with the minimum you are paying on another debt. Keep paying this debt until it is paid off, then take all of the payment money and apply it to another debt. Repeat this process until all of your debts are paid.

What makes this plan so effective is that with each debt that is paid off, there is more money applied to the next debt, so the time needed to pay it off is reduced because more money is applied to the principle of the debt.

As time goes by, the money directed towards paying off debt grows like a snowball rolling downhill.

If you decide to try the snowball method, you can attempt to pay down the debt with the highest interest rate first, then the second highest and so on. This makes sense from a mathematical point of view but not a psychological one. Although you may save money paying off debts with the highest interest rates first, it may not be possible to do so. You may find it depressing that you don't seem to be making any progress, especially if the first debt is taking too long to pay down. For this reason, it is better to pay off the lower balances first. It takes less time to pay off the smaller debts, and with each debt you pay off, you will grow in confidence. This confidence will help you follow through until the end. After all, the purpose of this method is to pay off your debts, and that is exactly what you will accomplish by paying off the debts from the smallest balance to largest balance of your debts.

Pay down your debt more quickly by cutting unnecessary expenses

To step up the pace to reach the day you become debt free, you can eliminate some of your expenses, and use this extra money to pay a debt. Using the snowball method, you should apply this extra money to the debt you are currently focused on. You don't have to make these expense cuts permanent, but only until you have paid off your debts. At that point you will have extra money to use as you wish. Getting out of debt is a sacrifice that you won't be making forever, but the more money you can free up to pay down your debts, the quicker the time frame will be to become debt free.

Sell off any assets you have that are not really needed

This is part of the same strategy as cutting expenses. If you have any assets that you don't need, you can sell them and apply this money to the debt you are currently paying down using the snowball method. Perhaps you have an extra car or a motorcycle that you don't really need. Anything you have that can be sold to use to pay down your debt will only hasten the day you are free from the bondage of debt.

Ron Charleston

Section 4

Bankruptcy

If it looks like you are facing a bankruptcy, do not delay filing. This is one of the mistakes people make with bankruptcy; they wait too long. This, along with filing themselves, are classic mistakes. Always consult with an attorney about your financial situation. The bankruptcy laws are more complicated than they appear. In fact, there are two types of personal bankruptcies. One is called Chapter 7 and the other Chapter 13. When the average person thinks of bankruptcy, they think that all of their debts will disappear, and they get a fresh start. To the extent that this happens, this is what Chapter 7 bankruptcy is about. However, there are certain debts that cannot be discharged. Examples of these types of debts are child support, student loans and many back taxes that are owed. Often a person thinks they will get a fresh start with no debt only to find out that they are not much better off after a bankruptcy. Always consult an attorney. You may discover that only a small portion of your debt can be discharged through a Chapter 7 bankruptcy filing.

If you have assets, you may be forced to sell them by a judge, but there are many assets that are protected when you go through a bankruptcy. This is another reason to speak to an attorney. In addition, an individual must qualify for a Chapter 7 bankruptcy in order to file.

If you do not qualify for a Chapter 7 filing, you may qualify for a Chapter 13 bankruptcy. This type of bankruptcy is a reorganization of your debt. Your debt is consolidated and often reduced into one payment that you send to a trustee. This person takes your payment and distributes it to your creditors. The bankruptcy is scheduled to be paid for a specific period of time. After this, it will be discharged, and you will no longer owe anybody any money.

Which path should you take?

If you qualify for a Chapter 7 bankruptcy, this may be the best path to take, but you should consult with an attorney. If you don't qualify for a Chapter 7 bankruptcy, but you do qualify for a restructuring of your debt under a Chapter 13 bankruptcy, this may be a better choice than using one of those debt consolidation companies that you see advertising on television and the Internet. Chapter 13 is debt consolidation, but it is done under the supervision of a court. You will not have to deal with debt collectors anymore and will be able to breathe easier with your personal finances. However, again, you should consult with an attorney. If you can't afford an attorney, rest assured, bankruptcy attorneys understand this, and payments can be made. I believe with a Chapter 13 filing, the attorney fee may be rolled into the debt consolidation, but an attorney can provide you with better information.

If you decide on bankruptcy, keep in mind that it will hurt your credit rating for seven to ten years, and it will probably be at least three years before you can get any more credit. But from this writer's point of view, it doesn't matter because you shouldn't be using credit anymore. There is no value in borrowing money.

If you do not qualify for bankruptcy, it is likely you have income, assets or a combination of the two that enable you to pay back the money you owe. If this is the case, you will want to consider paying down the debt yourself. Use whatever strategy you want, but pay off your debts, and once you are debt free, stay that way.

Ron Charleston

Section 5

Live Below Your Means

Once you have finally reached the point where you have paid off all of your debts, you will become one of the few Americans who are actually debt free. With a little discipline and some luck, you may be able to stay this way for the rest of your life. An important factor to staying out of debt is to build up a financial cushion. A little something extra to fall back on when life takes an unexpected turn. The key to doing this is living below your means.

It all starts with your budget

Everyone knows that a budget is important for your personal finances, but in order to live beneath your means, you have to know exactly how much money you're spending every month, and what your total expenses are to know how much you have left.

Once you have this information, you can begin to trim back your expenses to create a savings. You may have already done this in order to pay down your debt. In this case, you need only keep a portion of the money and save it for a rainy day.

But you must be careful. Once you have paid off your debt, there is going to be a temptation to simply spend your extra money on yourself. Although this is understandable, you need to begin saving as well.

Also, without a budget, there will be expenses that occur occasionally, and you won't have extra money for this. When these types of expenses show up, the temptation to go into debt will be easy, but you must avoid this by building your savings and not living paycheck to paycheck.

People are often not able to stick to their monthly budget, and it is often thought that the problem is fiscal discipline. The truth is that many people fail to stay within their budget because the budget was underestimated to begin with. There are many expenses that are forgotten and not accounted for in the monthly budget. When these expenses occur, people are caught short and must borrow the money. Examples of non-monthly expenses are care repairs, car registration, Christmas gifts, taxes and veterinarian services. You simply need to set aside enough money each month to pay for these expenses when the time comes to pay for them.

Keep in mind that no matter how hard you try to make an accurate budget, you will most likely forget one or more items the first time you make one. Don't let it get you down. Simply make the necessary adjustments. Over time, your budget will become more accurate.

Start reducing your expenses

Once you have an accurate budget and you have learned to live within your means, you can begin to cut back. There are a thousand ways to save money and I won't begin to list them here.

The best source of material to me, and the bible for saving money, is in a series of publications called the Tightwad Gazette. If memory serves, they are a compilation of newsletters by the same name. I think that there were at least three volumes available. You can buy them new or used. However, there are plenty of ideas on how to save money on the Internet as well. And there are other books in publication on the subject too. You probably can come up with your own ideas as well.

In general, anything you can buy used will save you a lot of money, and once you have left credit behind and start paying cash, you will begin to understand why cash is king. The deals you can get are an eye opener.

Section 6

No More Banks

I don't like banks. Years ago, or at least what I was taught in school, was that banks kept your deposits safe and paid you an interest rate. They then took this money and lent it out to businesses in the community and to people buying homes. Naturally, they charged more interest for the loans than the interest paid to depositors, but this is how they made their money. Maybe that was just a story told to school children, but it seems today that this is far from the way banks make their money. Now, it is all about fees. The more fees they can charge, the more profit they will make.

Here is a classic example of how big banks make money from the fees. If you have a checking account, you are likely to have a debit card associated with it. These big banks can get higher fees from debit card users than late fees on credit cards. If you go to use your debit card and you don't have enough money to cover the purchase, no problem. The bank will approve this purchase, and your account goes negative. Unless you make a deposit by the end of the day, the bank will hit you with an overdrawn penalty. In some cases this can be as high as $35. And this can result from a small purchase. Perhaps you lost track of exactly how much money you had left in your account. You use the card for a $15 dollar purchase with a $10 balance. This gets expensive quickly. Of course, it would be easy for the bank to decline payment, but there is simply too much profit to be made from these fees. This is only one of the many examples of how large banks rip off the consumer.

Another way a bank will gauge you is with ATM fees. With many bank accounts, the only way to avoid this is by using your bank's ATM machines. If not, you are charged a fee by the company that owns the ATM machine, as well as one by your bank. I have never understood this double fee. I understand a fee for using another company's ATM machine; after all, it's their machine, but getting charged by your own bank is like being charged because you're not showing loyalty. You're cheating on your bank. They should call it an infidelity fee. But seriously, I think this second fee is robbery.

Financial pundits on television will claim that people with low incomes are under served or under banked, but the truth is that they are victims of legal robbery. Most people of limited means are better off without a traditional bank account. Of course, without using a bank, your finances can get expensive. One problem that can happen without a bank account is cashing your paycheck. Assuming you get a paper check, without a bank account, you will have to pay a fee for a check cashing company to cash your paycheck.

If you have the need for the occasional paper check to be cashed, you should avoid using a paycheck cash business. Walmart has a check cashing service, and compared to most check cashing companies, their fees are reasonable. But if your place of employment allows for direct deposit, there is a good alternative to a checking account and avoiding check cashing services completely.

Prepaid debit cards

A prepaid debit is used just like you would a debit card that is linked to a checking account. This type of account functions the same as a checking account but with no checks. Like a checking account, you will have a bank account number and a routing number for the bank that issues the debit card. These two pieces of information can be given to your employer if they provide a direct deposit service. Your paycheck can be transferred directly to your account. When you use a prepaid debit card, it can be as cheap or cheaper than a checking account, but without the risk of predatory bank fees. They can be a good alternative to a checking account. However, there are a few things you need to be aware of.

1) Your are charged a fee to load more money on to your card. This is why it is important to have your paycheck loaded onto the card. When it is done this way, there is no charge. You can also use this same card for tax refunds or any other bank transfer. Remember, a prepaid debit card is a bank account, so you can always transfer money in the manner you would with a checking account. You can avoid loading fees with direct deposit.

2) You should avoid using ATM machines because it costs money to do so. Of course, this is true with a regular bank account, at least when the ATM machine is not a part of the bank's network. There is one way around this. There are many retail stores and supermarkets that allow you to get cash back from your purchase. This is a free way of getting the cash you need. But you can use your debit card for most purchases.

3) There is a monthly fee for a prepaid debit card, but it is often cheaper than a checking account, and without any minimum balance required. Monthly fees for prepaid debit cards vary, so you need to compare rates. Typically they are around $5.00. One popular card is Netspend. I happen to have experience with this card. Their monthly fee is $9.95, but if you have direct transfer, the monthly fee drops to $5.00. This is very reasonable. There is also a prepaid debit card available from Walmart

that I have heard is good too.

There has been a large growth in the market for prepaid debit cards, so there are more companies competing for your business than ever before. There are some prepaid debit cards with no monthly fee, while others have a network of ATM machines that are free to use. Still others allow you to load money on your card without a charge at certain financial locations. You should shop around for the card that suits your needs.

Of course, that still leaves the problem of needing the occasional check, especially if you need to pay your rent. In situations like this, a money order is a good substitute for a check. It's true, there is a cost to a money order, but if you are only buying one or two each month, it may be a cost effective approach. Money orders are available at any post office; they are low cost, and are recognized by all banks. So everyone will accept them.

Credit unions are the best alternative to a commercial bank

If you absolutely must have the services of a bank, at least for that occasional check, then I strongly recommend a credit union. Not everyone can get by with a prepaid debit card and the occasional money order. I understand this, but at the same time, I don't think it justifies the use of a bank. If at all possible, look for a credit union in your community. You can have both a checking account and a savings account at a credit union without the constant threat of banking fees hitting your account without warning.

Credit unions are different than banks

First and foremost, they do not operate for profit the way a bank does. A bank is owned by its stockholders, and they work to make as much profit as possible. Often, in the process of making a profit, the customer is a casualty. Credit unions, on the other hand, are owned by the depositors. Profits are put back into the credit union. The result is that the cost of having an account at a credit union is lower than a commercial bank. In some cases, you may be eligible for a free checking account. This is common with direct deposit from your employer. Credit unions commonly offer free checking accounts to students and seniors.

Once you have opened an account, you will become eligible for other services as well. Money orders are available through a credit union as well as Individual Retirement Accounts, money market accounts and sometimes safety deposit boxes. Most credit unions offer the same services as a commercial bank.

There are other benefits as well. Car loans have lower interest rates. Although I don't recommend financing a car, there are exceptions. You may have a chance to make more money at a new job, but you also need a car to get to this job. In a case such as this, where a car loan means an increase in income, it may make sense. But you need to get a loan with the lowest interest rate possible. This means an auto loan from a credit union, and you may be able to get a loan with no credit, especially if your employer provides direct deposit to your credit union account.

One drawback to a credit union

Unlike a commercial bank, you cannot simply open an account with a credit union. You must first meet certain eligibility requirements. Sometimes a credit union will be for those in certain professions such as teaching, the military or postal workers. Some private businesses offer a credit union. I was a member of a credit union years ago that I was eligible to join through my private sector employer. There are, however, other ways to become eligible. There are many credit unions where the only eligibility requirement is that you be a resident of a certain city or county. You will need to find the credit unions in your area and inquire about eligibility.

Another drawback to a credit union

Unlike large banks, the number of branches for a credit union are fewer in number. I really don't think this is too big of a problem because for me, there is little need to walk into a physical branch of a credit union. However, ATM machines are limited in number too, and this can be a problem. Remember, you will be charged fees when you use a debit card outside of your network. Some credit unions join up with others to form a larger network than what is possible with a single credit union.

However, even if there are limited ATM machines available, you can always adopt the strategy of using your credit union debit card for cash back at grocery stores and other retail outlets that allow cash back with a purchase.

If you do not qualify for a credit union

If there are no credit union possibilities in you area, then, and only then, I would consider a bank, but only a local bank. The more local the better. Sometimes there are banks that are located in a particular state or a certain area of a state, they are less likely to nickel and dime you with fees. Make sure they are FDIC insured, and you understand all of the requirements for the account as well as their schedule of fees. However, before going down this road, you should give a prepaid debit card a chance.

Section 7

Health Care

Earlier, I said that after you have paid off your debts, you could stay that way with discipline and some luck. The luck part is your health. Debts from medical bills can happen suddenly and pile up quickly. Medical bills are the leading cause of bankruptcy. Much of this problem can be addressed with good health coverage, but this is something that is slipping away from Americans. Low paying jobs do not have good health coverage, and many of them have none at all. With this in mind, I have outlined a few options that may help you if you are self-employed or do not have insurance coverage at your current job.

Health care for self-employed people is a big issue. There are many reasons you may become self-employed. In some situations, such as mine, it was never a choice, but simply one of survival after a layoff. But you may have decided to leave your job and start your own business. But whatever the situation, one of the biggest issues you will face is finding health care coverage.

The following are different ways to get health care coverage. Some of them may apply to your situation, while others may not.

COBRA

This is something that is usually available to those who have been laid off from a job that provided health care coverage. COBRA is an acronym for Consolidated Omnibus Budget Reconciliation Act and is a law that requires an employer to provide the recently laid off workers with medical insurance. This coverage is limited to a year and a half after you are laid off. When I lost my job years ago, I signed up for this plan. One thing that was shocking was the cost. I hadn't realized how much money my employer spent to pay for the cost of medical insurance. Under COBRA, I believe I was paying all of it.

If you can afford it, this may be a good option. And if you believe you will find another job in the next 18 months with a good health care plan, then using COBRA will prevent a lapse in your insurance coverage. Avoiding this can save you substantial money on premium costs.

https://www.shrm.org/templatestools/hrqa/pages/howlongdoescobralast.aspx

Marketplace exchanges

The Affordable Care Act, also known as Obamacare, allows certain insurance companies to compete for your business. The cost of this insurance is usually lower than what you will pay on your own, because the cost of the policy is partly paid by the federal government. The catch to this is that you may not qualify; however, if you do, it can be a good deal. I realized that this government program is controversial, but you need to swallow your political beliefs. This is about economic survival. The policy you buy through these private exchanges will only last a year, and then you will need to qualify again. And who knows? Laws can be changed, so this program may not be available in the future. But take what you can get today, and focus on protecting yourself and your family.

Medicaid

Medicaid is sometimes confused with Medicare, a medical insurance program for seniors. Medicaid is a program designed for the poor, and I have to mention it because of the erosion of the middle class. Many people have seen a reduction in their standard of living to the point where they have become poor and do not realize it. If you are not insured, and you have a low income, you may qualify for Medicaid. You must qualify with both income and assets. There are income levels that the federal government uses to determine poverty, and there are different poverty levels that depend upon the number of members of your household. You must also have few, if any, assets to qualify. Poverty is defined as low income and little wealth.

Under the Affordable Care Act, the income standards rose by a third. This makes it easier to qualify for Medicaid. The catch here is that there was a Supreme Court decision ruled that no state could be forced into this expansion of Medicaid. If you live in a state that opted into the expansion, you may find it easier to qualify. However, if you live in a state that has opted out of the Medicaid expansion, it is possible for you to be in the category where you have an income that is between the former standard for poverty and the new expanded figure.(100% to 133%). If this is true, you will not qualify for Medicaid in your state, and you will not qualify for the private exchanges because you don't make enough money. This is a tough place to be for low income earners. There are not too many options. You could move to another state, make more money, or make less money. But there may be a couple of other options, so read on.

Medicare

I have to include this for the sake of completeness. Most people know what Medicare is because they have been paying into it for years. This is something you will qualify for when you turn 65. The main thing to be said about Medicare is that it is the best deal for seniors, so you need to sign up for it as soon as you become eligible. Also, during the enrollment period, you need to consider buying a supplemental insurance policy. Medicare only pays approximately 80% of your medical bills. A good supplemental policy will help pay much of the rest of the bill. If you are too poor to buy a supplemental policy, you may qualify for Medicaid. If you are currently enrolled in Medicare, it is possible to use Medicaid as supplemental insurance if you qualify.

Purchase your own policy privately

Like most anything else in this country, you can simply buy your own medical insurance, privately. This is obvious to most people, but it is equally obvious that this is the most expensive option. There is one exception to this. The insurance industry calls it a catastrophic policy. These policies will have the lowest monthly premiums because they also have the highest deductibles. I had this type of policy after my COBRA coverage ran out. I remember, and this was years ago, my deductible was $5,000 a year. This meant that I would have to spend $5,000 out of my own pocket before the coverage kicked in. Even after the deductible was paid for, the policy would not cover everything. If I remember right, it was from $5,001 to $9,999 the policy covered 80%. $10,000 and more of medical bills and the policy would begin to cover 100%. This is why it is called catastrophic. It is only going to cover medical bills if something severe happens to you such as an accident or other health emergency that requires an extended stay at a hospital.

My experience with a catastrophic policy

A few months after my layoff, I purchased one of these insurance policies. This type of policy is great if you have assets to protect. After more than 20 years of working at the same company and working my way up from the bottom, I had accumulated a decent amount of assets that needed to be protected from large medical bills. Over time, I sold off many of these assets to simply survive as my income plunged. At a certain point, this type of policy no longer mattered. If my medical bills every exceeded the cost of a typical deductible for one of these catastrophic policies, I would be stuck with a medical bill I couldn't pay, and this would result in a bankruptcy. I could also save the premium money to use for health care costs. Bankruptcy never happened, because my health was good. Any minor ailments I had could be taken care of at a health clinic or quick care facility. Because I had no insurance, it was not cheap to go to these places, and any medical bill had to be paid in full, but the total cost was much cheaper than going to a private doctor. But again, during this time of my life, I was lucky I didn't get badly sick.

If you're married, get added to your spouse's health care coverage

This is common for many people. In some cases, one person may not have a good paying job, but the job has health coverage. If you lose your job, the natural thought is to get coverage on your spouse's policy. This is usually a smart move, but you still need to compare this to any other options you may have for medical insurance. Depending upon the amount of money your spouse is making, it may seem like your partner is simply working for health coverage. But you have to pool your money to survive, and you should look at the total financial picture for your household.

One last comment on health care

Health care costs can be devastating, and no matter how hard you try to stay healthy, there is always the possibility of incurring large medical bills. For some of us, preexisting health issues are a part of our lives, and represent a daily expense that will never go away. Economic survival in America means access to some form of health care, and this can be the toughest part of the equation. The ideas listed above are not complete; they only represent the most common solutions, and they do not apply to everyone. There are likely other possibilities, so keep researching and asking questions of friends and neighbors. You may discover a solution that will help you. But always remember, what is a solution today, may not be a solution tomorrow. Our nation is in a constant state of flux as we search for solutions to the health care problem, so stay alert to new possibilities to keep you and your loved ones protected.

Ron Charleston

Section 8

Expand Your Sources of Income

Please understand what I mean by expand your sources of income. I am not simply talking about increasing your income; you can do that by getting a promotion at work. But the money you earn from a single job can vanish overnight with a pink slip because the company is cutting back, relocating, or just going out of business. You need to have more than one income. In fact, the more sources of income you have, the better off you will be. If you were to lose one income, you will not be crippled by it. You might need to cut back on your expenses, but you won't be devastated by it.

Of course, the big question is how do you go about getting additional sources of income.

I could write an entire book on this subject, and that is just covering the things that have made me money since I lost my job and a career many years ago. Most of my sources of income have dried up or do not represent a significant percentage of my income any more. So it wouldn't be worth my time or yours to be specific about those sources of income. But by way of example, there was a three year period where I made a lot of money selling used books on eBay. There was good money in books before everybody starting doing it, and the prices for books fell flat.

I have done a many things that have made me good money, and when things are going good, I try to ride these horses for everything they're worth. I know, of course, that no income source will last a lifetime, at least in the area of self-employment, so I am always looking for new sources of income. Right now, I am writing my first book. Perhaps this will make me money and lead to more books, but perhaps not. The point is, I am always looking for a new fishing hole.

Multiple streams of income – at least two sources

If you are fortunate to have a job that gives you a steady paycheck, you need to have something going on the side. Employment in America is simply not as steady as it was years ago, and it may never be that way again. No matter what job you have, it is always safe to assume that a layoff is only a day away. So what do you do? Where do you start?

Focus on work you can do out of your home on your own time. The idea of having a side business is nothing original, but it is an essential part of survival in today's economy. An additional benefit is that it may be possible to get wealthy off a side business. No one ever got rich working for someone else, and if you are always on the lookout for new opportunities, you may hit upon something that is lucrative. At least lucrative enough to launch yourself into the world of the upper middle class.

Making money online

As I have gotten older, I have developed health issues that have affected my mobility, and it is for this reason that I make all of my money online. There is a wide range of methods of making money online. The following is a brief look at three ways to do this with a few words of warning. All three of these methods take no upfront investment other than your time.

Content writing

Every website or blog you visit on the Internet is filled with articles and other information. What you may not know is that much of this written content is purchased. There are several ways that this is done, but one popular way is to buy it from a company that specializes in producing it. A business or website owner specifies what they need and then a content company has their writers produce the required content. If you like writing, it doesn't cost anything to start doing this type of work.

A word of caution: Not all content sites are equal. Some of them are not very professional, and their pay rates usually reflect this. Getting payment for your work can also be an issue. But among those companies that are dependable, you can make a few dollars writing. The money is not great, but the practice in writing on a daily basis can lead to private clients, and a career as a freelance writer. If you are interested, the following are a few sites that I have found to be good.

Textbroker

Writers Domain

Crowd Content

Content Runner

Some of these content sites may already have enough writers, and you must wait for them to take on new workers. The best ones are usually the hardest to join up with. Some of them even have grammar tests. But you can still get your feet wet with other content writing sites that have lower paying rates. Just remember not to commit too much time into a particular company until you get a feel for what type of business you are dealing with. You also want to work with a company that has been in business for several years. These types of online companies have come and gone over the years, and you don't want to get burned by one if they go out of business and still owe you money.

Audio Transcription

This is a needed service and is something you can do from your home. Basically, you receive an audio file and transcribe what you hear into text. There are different sources of audio that people want this service for. Speeches, lectures, podcasts are only three examples. I did this work for a while. The entry level pay isn't very good, but if you stick with it, there is the possibility of making a living at it. Some of the high end work involves medical transcription work, but this takes specialized training. However, the required classes are not extensive, and if you find that you like audio transcription work, you can pursue it further. Medical transcription being only one possibility.

The best way to start is sign up with a company that acts as a broker. These companies essentially have the same business model as content writing companies. They solicit orders from clients that need transcription work, and then offer it to a group of subcontractors. You are working for yourself, but will get paid by the transcription company when your work is approved. This is a good way to start in this field because you don't have to go looking for customers, and you can gain valuable experience. I worked for several different companies years ago when I started out. Each company has its own guidelines and rules for transcription, so you will need to be well versed in their rules.

One example of a company I did transcription work for was Speechink. Most of the work was transcribing interviews of people involved in car accidents for attorneys. For legal reasons, all words, even sounds, had to be transcribed. As I wrote this, I was curious to see if this company is still around. They are, but they are now called Speechpad Worker. I remember having to take a test; my score was high enough that I qualified to do work for them. I imagine most of these companies require you to take a test. The pay wasn't high, but it was a good entry point for audio transcription work. At times, the work was tedious, but what work isn't? Eventually, I gave up transcription work, but it was due to a hearing problem I developed.

If you find that you like this kind of work, you will want to invest in transcription software and a foot pedal. This latter piece of equipment is connected to your computer with a USB port. It allows you to start and stop an audio file, so you can keep both hands on your keyboard to transcribe. It is well worth the money to buy one because your productivity will increase. As far as software, there are various programs for this type of work. Some are cheap; others are more expensive. These programs allow you to download a file, and then change the volume, bass, treble and can filter out some of the noise. I can't remember the name of the program I used, but I do remember it was free; however, the free version did not have many of the options that the full version had, but the full version was available at a reasonable price.

Fiverr.com – Offer your services

This is a website where you can offer a variety of services for $5. That may not sound like much, and in truth, it isn't, but many people have made good money by offering extras or add-ons to their services. At this website you offer a basic service and that is all that a person is required to purchase, but if the extras are attractive, the average order will be much higher. Also, if you can do the five dollar jobs quickly and to a high standard, the money may still be worth it. It depends upon how much money you are looking to make. You can browse the website to see if there are services that you may be able to provide given your skills. I have purchased many jobs at this site. Maybe, someday I'll buy from you.

Making money locally

There are many things you can do locally to make a few extra dollars, and over time, many of them can become a significant source of income. The following is just a short list that is based upon friends and relatives I know who have started businesses on the side.

Multi-level marketing (MLM)

I have to mention this because it is so popular, but the entire area of multi-level marketing (MLM) is suspicious to me. The most famous company in this area is Amway. This type of business is one in which you make money through commission by selling a product and by recruiting new members, earning a portion of your income from the sales your recruits makes. As long as more than half of the income paid by the company is earned by selling a product, this type of company is legal, but when less than half of the income is from selling a product, the government deems it a pyramid scheme. You are looking for legitimate ways to make money. Anything that is suspicious or even on the edge of illegal should be avoided. But even the legitimate MLM firms often require you to purchase large minimum orders with no return privileges, so you can get stuck with a lot of unsold inventory.

Auto mechanic work

If you have certain skills in this area, you may be able to make some money on the side. You don't have to be a professional mechanic, only have some experience doing certain work. And it doesn't take any investment, other than getting the word out. Your clients can spend money on the parts that are needed while you make the repairs. It can be something as simple as replacing the starter. An individual has a new starter for his or her car, but has no experience or tools needed to remove the old one and install the new one.

Computer repair work

So many of the problems people have with their computers can be traced to a malware program that has infected their system, or improperly installed software. In short, it is seldom a hardware issue. But even when it is, some hardware issues are easy to fix. For example, installing a new hard disk. Adding additional memory or other computer upgrades are fairly simple. If you have skills with computers, this may be a good way to make extra money. You may need some tools and diagnostic software for this work, but these are easily obtained and are not expensive.

Handyman

This is a broad category, but basically includes the many things homeowners need but are simple enough not to require a licensed contractor. One good example is installing a garbage disposal. If you have done this before, as I have, then you know it is not that difficult. But if a homeowner doesn't want to do it themselves, they can have a handyman do it. A plumber isn't necessary for this type of work, but a plumber will be expensive. You can save a homeowner money by offering this type of service. Other work that can be done includes house painting, cleaning rain gutters, minor roof repair, replacing a faucet, installing a new toilet and installing ceiling fans.

The ideas listed above only scratch the surface of work that you can do locally, part time, and often without a license.

Avoid borrowing to finance your business

You also want to avoid using any credit to make money. Let the fruit of your labor produce the value that creates your income. When you start buying things on credit to resell, you will wind up in debt all over again, or get into debt for the first time. And this only happened because you were trying to generate an income. There are times when you need to spend money to make money; this is simply an investment. But you need to invest your own cash, and not borrow to pay for anything.

A New Beginning

Conclusion

After you get your personal finances straightened out and you are headed towards a debt free life, you need to begin to search for additional sources of income. This in no way implies that you should give up your day job, but only recognizes the reality of today's work environment. There is no such thing as job security. Part-time work with few benefits and low wages are the greatest growth areas in the U.S. Economy. Even if you have a good paying job, you could lose it in the immediate future. The trick to having a stable income is diversity. You need to have several sources of income, so if one source dries up, you still have money flowing into your pocket.

It is likely that some of what you've read is information you already were aware of, but what is important is that you take action. The United States economy is not likely to change in the near future or even for the rest of our lives. You must adapt your personal finances to this new reality. You can still enjoy the fruit of your labor, but like many of us, including myself, you will need to lower your expectations for material possessions, and embrace life's experiences more. Get more enjoyment out of life from doing rather than having. As we get older, our fondest memories are not what we owned, but the experiences we had, and usually these good times were spent with family and friends.

Once you have freed yourself from the credit trap and have become debt free, you will begin to experience life in a better way. Always enjoy the fruit of your labor, and never forget how precious your time is that you spend with the ones you love.

I wish you the best

Ron Charleston

About The Author

For more than 20 years, Ron Charleston worked in the field of electrical engineering, but after a sudden layoff, he found himself unemployed and with few career options in sight. This led to a new outlook on his personal finances and income generation. Today, Ron is self-employed, and makes his income exclusively from online activity.

Ron Charleston

Other publications from Teela Books

Sports and Horse Racing Betting Systems That Work! by Ken Osterman

The book contains some of the best sports betting systems from Ken Osterman. These are systems that he has used himself successfully at both racetracks and sports books. The rules for each system are clearly explained and the systems are explained clearly so it is understood why they work. Tips for improving these systems are also provided.

There are 10 systems in this book that cover horse racing, football and baseball. Here is a list of the systems with the sport that is covered and the title of the system.

Horse racing

Quarter Horse - The Hidden Speed Horse Angle

Thoroughbred - Best Jockey – Long shot Method

Thoroughbred - Bet the Fastest Horse

Thoroughbred - Show a profit down under

Harness - The qualifier advantage

Harness - Morning Line Overlay

Sports Betting

NFL Football - The Injured Star

NFL Football - The Hat Trick

Baseball - The AAA Surprise

Baseball - The Underdog Advantage

This book is currently available:

In Kindle format on Amazon:

http://www.amazon.com/dp/B00JTMWDNM

It is also available on iBooks, Barnes & Noble, Kobo, Inktera, Scribd, 24Symbols, and Tolino.

It is also available in Paperback on Amazon

http://www.amazon.com/dp1507800142

The Path to Harness Racing Handicapping Profits by Douglas Masters

The Secrets of Harness Race Profits Revealed!

This book represents three decades of handicapping and betting harness races and is a summary of observations that are important to being a winning player. This book summarizes the conclusions on what made the author a winning player. There is no magic formula to become a winning player and the author is the first to say that there is more than one road to profits. This book is the road taken by Doug Masters to becoming a winning player. Becoming a winning player is part art and part skill, so it is impossible to summarize it as a mechanical method; however, Doug attempts to outline his process in the second half of the book.

This book may be difficult for beginning harness handicappers to read because it does not explain any basic terminology. There are, however, glossaries of harness racing terms online as well in the racing programs of harness tracks.

There are no winning examples in this book.

This is a quote from the author in the introduction.

"You will find no past performances listed in this book; this is intentional. Anyone who has been around harness racing for even a few years has probably read various books and publications offering a handicapping system. All of them will have examples of how a handicapping system or angle picked a winner. Anyone can do this, especially when so many of these authors are working backwards from the winner. To me, it is simply a waste of time. And besides, only a mediocre or inexperienced handicapper is going to believe there is a single path to success in wagering. This book consists of my observations of the sport and how it relates to my own handicapping perspective. If you are looking for a system that represents some sort of absolute truth, you're looking in the wrong place."

Topics include: Handicapping Factors, Drivers, Horse Form, Speed, Pace, Class, Post position, Track, Statistics, Betting multiple racetracks.

This book is currently available:

In Kindle format on Amazon:

http://www.amazon.com/dp/B00I5B13MU

It is also available on iBooks, Barnes & Noble, Kobo, Inktera, Scribd, 24Symbols, and Tolino.

It is also available in Paperback on Amazon

Type 2 Diabetes: From diagnosis to a new way of life

by Matthew Lashley

From the author

This book tells the story of how my diabetic condition was discovered, my denial of the condition, then the work done to get my glucose level to levels that are close to normal. There is no magic solution to treating type 2 diabetes, but I hope the information that I gathered and applied to my own life may be helpful to everyone struggling with type 2 diabetes. There is no cure, and I will have this condition the rest of my life. However, type 2 diabetes can be treated and controlled with the proper approach and lifestyle changes. You can have a better quality of life with a diet that is compatible with this disease.

Topics include:

From denial to self-blame

How I found out what type 2 diabetes was

Acceptance and getting down to work

Medication

Type 2 diabetes is a serious illness

How many carbohydrates per day should the limit be?

My target glucose levels

Foods to eat and foods to avoid

The importance of fiber in the diet

Eating out at restaurants

Is the damage from type 2 diabetes reversible?

Can type 2 diabetes be prevented?

This book is currently available:

In Kindle format on Amazon:

http://www.amazon.com/dp/B00IRJ9L1K

It is also available on iBooks, Barnes & Noble, Kobo, Inktera, Scribd, 24Symbols, and Tolino.

It is also available in Paperback on Amazon

http://www.amazon.com/dp/1508826005

The Quick and Dirty NFL Football Handicapping Method By Ken Osterman

The purpose of this book is to explain a fundamental approach to making a profit betting on professional football games, especially for those with little time to handicap them.

This method will help you find an overlay in the point spread using the simplest and quickest method possible.

The Quick and Dirty NFL Football Handicapping Method teaches you how to create your own point spread for each game in the NFL.

Table of Contents

Money Management

Improving this method

Mistakes to Avoid

Conclusion

This book is currently available:

In Kindle format on Amazon:

http://www.amazon.com/dp/B00NX9X81I

It is also available on iBooks, Barnes & Noble, Kobo, Inktera, Scribd, 24Symbols, and Tolino.

It is also available in Paperback on Amazon

Betting on Major League Baseball

The Underdog Method By Ken Osterman

The essence of any good baseball handicapping system is to find games to bet on that will result in long-term profits. In other words, finding overlays. The Underdog Method uses an approach to not only find these good bets, but does so by creating a money line that can be compared to the one offered by sports books.

Author and sports gambler, Ken Osterman, explains this system in an easy-to-understand way, and then uses an entire day of baseball games as examples. Each game is handicapped per the rules of the Underdog Method, and then a betting line is created. This line is compared to a specific sports book's money line. It is then decided, based upon specific rules, whether a good bet exists or not.

Although demonstrating the effectiveness of any betting system is limited in a book, the approach to Major League Baseball betting using the Underdog System is significantly different than the simple angles and methods seen elsewhere.

This book is currently available:

In Kindle format on Amazon:

http://www.amazon.com/dp/B01220NL8I

It is also available on iBooks, Barnes & Noble, Kobo, Inktera, Scribd, 24Symbols, and Tolino.

It is also available in Paperback on Amazon

http://www.amazon.com/dp/1515180646

Free Things To Do on the Las Vegas Strip

A Self-Guided Tour By Matt Lashley

The Strip is world famous and not only for the casinos, but also for the many things to see and do. Of course, a lot of what you can do here costs money, but there are a number of things to do that are free.

This book is a self-guided tour, taking you step by step down the Strip to visit all of the notable free things to do. This excludes most of the photo opportunities, because the entire length of the strip is filled with places to take a photo of you, your friends and relatives. Only a few places of interest, directly in our travel path, are mentioned. Also, shopping sites have been excluded except for three unique stores of interest on the Strip.

The trip begins at the Welcome to Fabulous Las Vegas sign and ends in the downtown portion of Las Vegas Blvd. This is the old section of Las Vegas and is not considered a part of the Strip. I have included it to provide a complete Las Vegas experience.

This book is currently available:

In Kindle format on Amazon:

http://www.amazon.com/dp/B01EW6DWXY

It is also available on iBooks, Barnes & Noble, Kobo, Inktera, Scribd, 24Symbols, and Tolino.

It is also available in Paperback on Amazon

http://www.amazon.com/dp/1533524084

Stealth Betting Systems for Winning at Casinos by Luke Meadows

Stop Losing and Start Winning in Las Vegas casinos!

Author and casino gambler, Luke Meadows, explains his betting methods he uses in Las Vegas casinos in an easy-to-understand way. There are casino systems for the games of roulette, craps, blackjack, Let It Ride, and Keno. Mr. Meadows is convinced that your best chance of winning is small wins using smart gambling systems, and to do this without bringing attention to yourself – a stealth mode of casino gambling.

In all of this time Luke, like most of us, has experienced both winning and losing. Over time, his trips to Las Vegas have produced more profits than losses. The reason for this is his method of gambling at casinos. A method that he has honed and fine-tuned to the point where he has the best chance of winning, while at the same time, keeping his losses low.

This book is currently available:

In Kindle format on Amazon:

http://www.amazon.com/dp/B01KGSN63S

It is also available on iBooks, Barnes & Noble, Kobo,

Inktera, Scribd, 24Symbols, and Tolino.

It is also available in Paperback on Amazon

http://www.amazon.com/dp/1537175939

For the latest information about our publications, along with articles by some of our authors, please

visit our website at

http://www.teela-books.com

www.ingramcontent.com/pod-product-compliance
Lightning Source LLC
Chambersburg PA
CBHW070132210526
45170CB00013B/836